Jazz Piano Vocabulary

Volume 2
The Dorian Mode

by Roberta Piket

With additional material available
on-line at www.muse-eek.com

Muse Eek Publishing Company
New York, New York

Copyright © 2003 by Roberta Piket. All rights reserved

ISBN 189094498X

No part of this publication may be reproduced, stored in a
retrieval system, or transmitted, in any form or by any means,
electronic, mechanical, photocopying, recording, or otherwise,
without the prior written permission of the publisher.

Printed in the United States

This publication can be purchased from your local bookstore or by contacting:
Muse Eek Publishing Company
P.O. Box 509
New York, NY 10276, USA
Phone: 212-473-7030
Fax: 212-473-4601
http://www.muse-eek.com
sales@muse-eek.com

Table Of Contents

Acknowledgements	*iv*
About the Author	*v*
Foreword	*vi*
How to use this book	*vii*
Introduction To The Dorian Mode	10
Dorian Modes With Fingerings Plus Left Hand Chord Voicings	13
Other Ways To Practice The Dorian Mode	18
Examples Of Melodic Lines Using The Dorian Mode	22
Your Ideas	25
A Jazz Etude On *So What* Changes	29
Further Exploration	31

Acknowledgments

The author gratefully acknowledges Bruce Arnold for his invaluable feedback and Muse Eek Publishing for the opportunity to reach an appropriate audience with this book.

I would also like to thank all of my students over the past twenty years from whom I have learned a great deal, and all of my former teachers for the information and encouragement I have received from them.

Special thanks to Billy Mintz for his support and musical inspiration.

About the Author

Roberta Piket is from Queens, NY. Her father, composer Frederick Piket, gave her her first piano lessons when she was seven years old. Roberta began playing seriously in her early teens, studying jazz piano with Walter Bishop, Jr and classical piano with Vera Wels. After graduating from prestigious Hunter College High School, she entered the joint double-degree program at Tufts University and the New England Conservatory of Music, earning a Bachelor's Degree in Computer Science from the former and a Bachelor's Degree in Jazz Studies from the latter. During this time she studied privately with Fred Hersch, Stanley Cowell, Jim McNeely and Bob Moses. Soon after graduation Roberta returned to New York City to devote herself to music full-time, which she has done ever since. In New York, she studied for six years with Richie Beirach and also studied briefly with Sofia Rosoff.

Roberta has performed professionally as a sidewoman with David Liebman, Rufus Reid, Michael Formanek, Lionel Hampton, Mickey Roker, Harvey Wainapel, Eliot Zigmund, Billy Mintz, and the BMI/New York Jazz Orchestra, and has twice been a featured guest on *Marian McPartland's Piano Jazz*, on National Public Radio.

Roberta has taught at Long Island University and has several private students at the Berkeley-Carroll School in Brooklyn. She has also held master classes and/or clinics at the Eastman School of Music, Rutgers University, Duke University, as well as many other institutions in the U.S., Europe, and Japan.

Roberta has six CDs as a leader which have frequently made the jazz magazines' yearly top ten lists. She currently leads two bands: The *Roberta Piket Trio* and *Alternating Current*. *Piano & Keyboard* recently called Roberta "one of the most accomplished and inventive young jazz pianists currently working on the scene."

More information about Roberta's music can be found at her web sites: www.RobertaJazz.com and www.AlternatingCurrent.info.

Foreword

Many instrumentalists wish to pursue jazz improvisation, but are intimidated because they don't know what notes to play over chord changes, beyond the chord tones themselves. Frequently students who do know what scales they need to learn in order to play over changes are unable to internalize this information to the point of being able to use the scales in an actual playing situation. They may have difficulty learning the notes because they are unsure of what fingerings to use, or they may not have had enough guidance in making the transition from *playing* the scales to *applying* them in a playing situation.

This book provides specific details on practicing the Dorian mode in all twelve keys and applying it to jazz improvisation. You will also find ideas on how to create sequences and melodic patterns utilizing the Dorian mode, an original Dorian mode etude, and, since fingering is often an issue for less experienced pianists, fingerings for every scale and exercise in the book. The goal is to provide you with enough guidance to work confidently on your own so that you become comfortable using the Dorian mode to improvise.

This book is part of a series (available as e-books or in paper format) that will focus on learning and applying jazz scales in order to give you the vocabulary and skill to become a fluid jazz improvisor.

Muse Eek Publishing has created a website with a FAQ forum for this book. If you get stuck, or have questions or feedback, please contact me at Roberta@muse-eek.com and I will be happy to respond in the forum.

Roberta Piket
Brooklyn, New York

How To Use This Book

This series of books assumes that you know how to read music and that you have a basic understanding of major scales. If you need to brush up on your note-reading or diatonic (major and minor) scales, there are lessons on this topic in the members area of the publisher's website. If you find anything in this book confusing, please visit the Muse Eek web site at www.muse-eek.com first and check the FAQ section for this book to see if your question has already been answered. If not, use the form on the website to e-mail your questions.

A note on terminology: Occasionally the word *scale* will be used in this book interchangeably with the word *mode*. Generally I will only use the word *scale* when discussing general concepts such as scale tones or sequencing through a scale. When discussing a specific mode (such as D Dorian, for example) I will use the word *mode*.

The purpose of this book is to help you improve your ability to improvise using the Dorian mode. Since you are learning a new skill, reading the book and understanding the material intellectually are not enough. It is critical that you practice the modes and examples repeatedly until you have mastered them. Execute each example at the piano slowly and carefully to begin. Increase your tempo gradually as your ability increases.

You may wish to use a metronome to be certain that you are not slowing down on difficult passages. If you are able, try putting the metronome on the "two and four"; that is, the second and fourth beats of each measure. This emphasis on the "weak" beats instead of the "strong" first and third beats is part of what gives jazz its unique rhythmic character. If it is too difficult for you to play with the metronome on two and four, then first learn the scales with the metronome on the quarter note and then, after you are comfortable with the notes, try the "two and four" again. Eventually it will get easier to feel the music this way and your sense of rhythm will become stronger and more sophisticated.

This book contains a great deal of material. You will not be able to learn everything in the book in one sitting. In fact, depending on your background, and how much time you have to dedicate to the piano, it may take you anywhere from a few weeks to several months or more to truly master the exercises in this book. Spend as much time as you need on each page before moving on to the next page.

Consistency is critical. Even if you have less time on some days than on other days, it is extremely important that you refresh your memory almost every day until the material is completely engrained. If you do this, you will find that you will progress much more quickly and will save yourself a great deal of frustration.

Play through each exercise smoothly and evenly. As you master each exercise you should gradually increase the tempo while still maintaining complete control. This will help you to develop good habits which will remain with you when you start playing more technically challenging music.

In the same vein, it is also a good idea to go back to previous material even while moving forward through the book. This will help reinforce what you've already learned, thus enabling you to build on it. For example, if you have learned the first six Dorian modes and are working on the seventh, you may want to play through the first six at least once a day until they become second nature so that you don't forget them.

Swung Eighth Notes

Each mode is presented in an eighth note pattern (resolving to a quarter note at the top and bottom) to allow for an even four-bar phrase as the scale ascends and descends. If you are comfortable doing so, try to play each exercise with *swung eighth notes* so that this type of feel has a chance to become second nature to you. In swung (or "swinging") eighth notes, the first eighth note in a pair of eight notes is held twice as long as the second eighth note, giving the notes a relaxed triplet feel. Eighth notes are almost always interpreted in jazz music as *swung*. For example, note the following phrase:

In a jazz context, this would actually be played as:

Example 1

Since the concept of "swing" is such an elusive one, a sound file illustrating this example has been provided on the Muse Eek website under this book's title.

Note: Although jazz musicians generally interpret eighth notes with a swing feel, two exceptions to this are Brazilian jazz and Latin jazz where it is understood that the eight note is straight (that is, not swung).

Order of Presentation

The exercises and sample melodies are ordered by key using the *circle of fifths*. The circle of fifths means that we progress through all the keys by moving either up or down in perfect fifths from one key to the next. Only by moving up or down in fifths can we go through all the keys without repeating any key.

In this book we will progress down in fifths, from D Dorian to G Dorian to C Dorian, etc., until we arrive at the last mode, A Dorian. (We start with D Dorian for simplicity's sake: as is the case with its parent scale, C Major, D Dorian has no sharps or flats.)

Fingering

Often inexperienced pianists find it difficult to know which finger to use on which key. The fingerings that are provided in this book are intended to keep you from "running out of fingers" as you play ascending and descending lines.

Fortunately, fingering notation for piano is standardized throughout all genres of music. The thumb of each hand is always "1", and the pinky is always "5". If you can remember this then you will quickly become proficient at applying the correct fingerings as you learn to play a passage of written music.

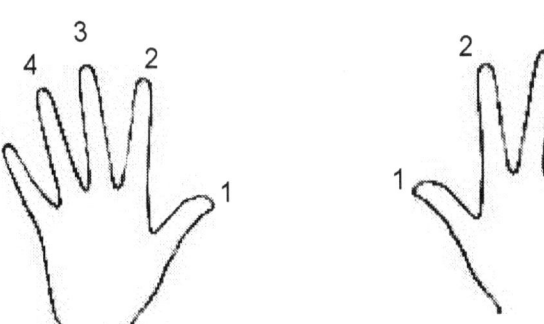

Particularly if you are self-taught, some of these fingerings may at first seem awkward. Give yourself a chance to get used to them. After learning them, if something still feels awkward, you can change it. Everyone's hand is different. However, don't assume they don't work if they feel "funny" the first time you try them. Practice them slowly, making sure to apply them accurately and consistently. Only by applying the correct fingerings every time you play will using them become automatic. Eventually, with enough experience, you will be able to determine the correct fingering on your own.

Introduction To The Dorian Mode

The modes that developed in Europe during the Medieval period are surprisingly useful in jazz improvisation. These modes are sometimes known as the "Church modes" because they evolved through the use of Gregorian chant, the sacred monophonic music of Europe's Catholic Church during this period. The Church modes are derived from the major scale. That is, each mode has the same notes as the major scale, but each mode starts and ends on a different note from the major scale. The seven modes that we use in jazz are: Ionian, Dorian, Phrygian, Lydian, Mixolydian, Aeolian, and Locrian.

This book is concerned with the Dorian mode. Below we will see how the notes of the Dorian mode fit over a minor seven chord, making this mode a useful tool for improvising on this chord.

The Dorian mode can be derived by starting and ending on the second note of a major scale. For example, the D Dorian mode starts on D, and contains all the notes in the C major scale from D to D:

D Dorian Mode

Because the D Dorian mode uses the notes of the C Major scale, C Major is referred to as the *parent scale of D Dorian*. By knowing the parent scale of a mode, it is easy to figure out the notes that belong to that mode. As another example, if we want to figure out how to play a G Dorian mode, we would first need to understand that G is the second degree of F Major, making F major the parent scale of G Dorian:

G Dorian Mode

Understanding the relationship of the Dorian mode to its parent scale will help you understand the mode's use and will make it easier to learn the notes of each mode. However, this is merely an intermediate step. The goal is to hear and relate to the D Dorian mode *as* a D Dorian mode, *not* as a

C major scale starting on D. If you do not learn to think and hear beyond C major when you play D Dorian, you are adding an extra step which will interfere with your ability to hear and react instantaneously to whatever chord you encounter when improvising. (If you have trouble hearing the modes and chords and how they relate to each other you may find it helpful to investigate one or more of the ear-training books on the Muse Eek website.)

Another way to think of the Dorian mode is in terms of its sequence of whole steps and half steps. (A half step is the distance between two notes that are right next to each other on the piano, such as A and B flat, or B and C. A whole step is simply two half steps. Major and minor scales, and the modes derived from these scales, always consist of combinations of these two intervals. For a more detailed explanation of these fundamental music theory concepts please visit the members area of the Muse Eek website.) Thus the pattern of steps for any Dorian mode in any key is the same:

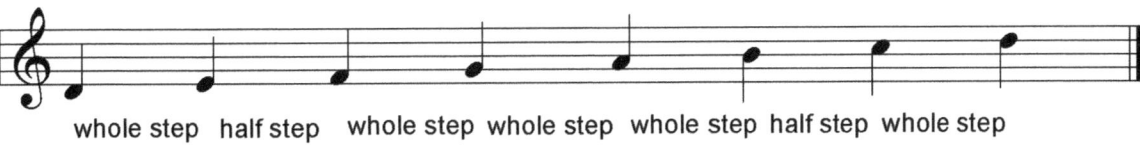

whole step   half step   whole step   whole step   whole step   half step   whole step

Relating the Dorian mode to the minor seven chord

If we consider the notes of the Dorian mode in terms of how they relate to a minor seven chord, we have (in ascending order) the root, the natural ninth, the third, the eleventh, the fifth, the sixth (or 13th), and the seventh of the chord.

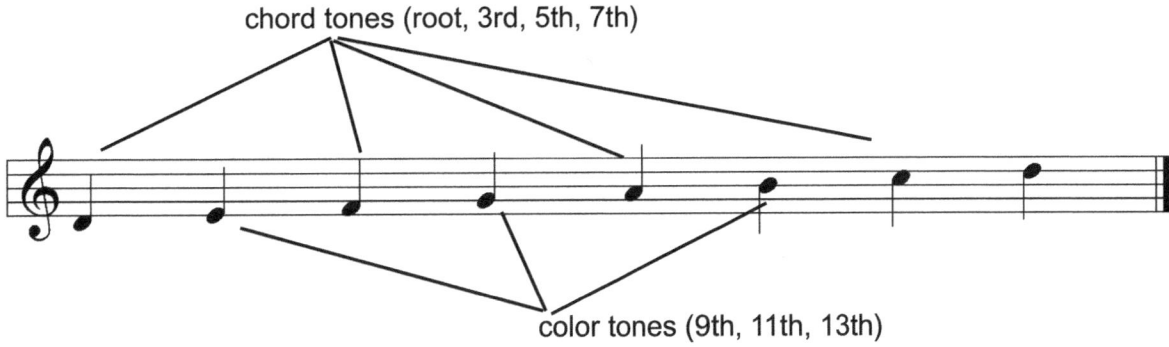

These relationships are, of course, the same for any Dorian mode. Therefore, any Dorian mode can be used to improvise over its corresponding minor seven chord. For example, a G Dorian Mode can be used to play over a G minor seven chord, an A Dorian mode can be used over an A minor seven chord, etc.

The upper extensions of the chord (that is, the 9th, 11th, and 13th) are known as *color tones*. They add shading to the chord that makes it more interesting. For a more detailed explanation of scale color tones, please go to the members' area of the Muse Eek website.

Left hand chord voicings

Once you are comfortable playing the modes in your right hand, the next step is to play the corresponding minor seven chord in the left hand while playing the mode in the right hand.

A left hand chord voicing is provided for you to accompany yourself while playing the corresponding mode in the right hand. The chord voicing uses the 3rd, 5th, 7th and 9th of the minor seven chord. For example:

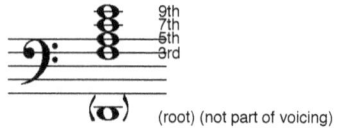

D-7 left hand voicing

This type of "rootless" voicing is useful to learn, because when you are playing with a bass player in a real-world situation, it is not always necessary to play each chord's root. The bass player will do that for you (usually).

For some of the left hand voicings, the order of the notes has been changed (inverted) so that the left hand will not sound too high or too low on the keyboard. For example, in a G minor seven chord, voicing the chord tones in order (from the 3rd up) will get in the way of the right hand. However, if we invert the chord so that the bottom two notes (the third and 5th) are placed on top of the 7th and 9th, then there will be more room for the right hand:

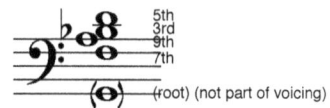

G-7 left hand voicing

Additional left hand voicing possibilities are provided on the Muse Eek web site in the members' area.

Dorian Modes with Fingerings Plus Left Hand Chord Voicings

Practice Tips

To begin, practice each mode in the right hand, up two octaves and down two octaves, paying attention to the fingering provided. (Right hand fingering is notated above each note of the scale.) You may find it useful to say each note out loud as you play. Even better for your ear is to try and sing the notes of each mode while playing.

The reason why you should initially focus on learning each mode in your right hand is that once you learn the notes you will be accompanying yourself with the appropriate chord in your left hand. However, for technical purposes and to provide textural variety in your soloing it can be useful to practice the modes with both hands. For this purpose, left hand fingerings for each Dorian mode are provided (below each note), and some sound files with examples of two-handed line playing are provided on the Muse Eek website under this book's title.

Adding the left hand chord voicing

After you learn the mode you will be ready to add the chord voicing in the left hand. The bass note in parentheses below the chord indicates the root of the chord. While you would not play this note in an actual playing situation, it is useful to hear the root when practicing. Play the root with your left hand and sustain it with the damper (sustain) pedal, then lift your hand and play the rootless voicing as written. While holding this chord with your left hand, take your foot off the damper pedal and play the mode in your right hand. This technique will help you hear the chord from the bottom up, allowing you to get its tonality in your ear. It will also enable you to aurally relate the mode to the chord.

Dynamics

Keep in mind that the left hand is *accompanying* the right hand. Therefore, the left hand should be a bit softer than the right hand. At first it may seem difficult to coordinate your hands in this way, but if you try to *hear* the right hand melody louder, as opposed to merely trying to play *harder*, then eventually you will naturally begin to emphasize the melody more.

Swung Eight Notes, Articulation and Phrasing

Playing these scales with a swung eighth note feel (as explained in the "How To Use This Book" section), will help you to develop a more authentically "jazz" rhythmic feel.

As you become more comfortable with the actual notes of each scale and chord, you should begin to focus more on the subtleties of articulation. Each scale should be played legato, meaning that the notes are connected. Many jazz piano students make the mistake of trying to play too staccato, because of the percussive nature of jazz. However, do *not* use the damper or sustain pedal when playing medium tempo or faster jazz eighth note lines. This is another common error made by students. This dichotomy is one of the biggest challenges of jazz piano: to articulate your melodic lines smoothly so that each note in a phrase is connected, but not to allow the notes to run together and get "mushy". Play each phrase legato, but make sure that each eighth note is played exactly in time and articulated cleanly.

Most Western musicians are trained to emphasize the strong beats in each measure. This means that, outside of jazz, the second eighth note in a pair (the "and") is considered a weaker beat and is given less emphasis than the first eighth note. In jazz, however, as mentioned earlier, it is the emphasis on the weak beats that provides the forward motion and rhythmic interest unique to this form of music. This does not mean that when you solo you must emphasize every upbeat. Doing this all the time will make your playing sound mechanical. However, as an exercise, you may wish to *practice* these scales while accenting all the upbeats. This will help improve your jazz rhythmic feel and generally strengthen your sense of rhythm, time and articulation.

An illustration of this practice technique follows. Note the accents on every second eighth note. An audio file of this example can be found on the Muse Eek website under this book's title.

Example 2

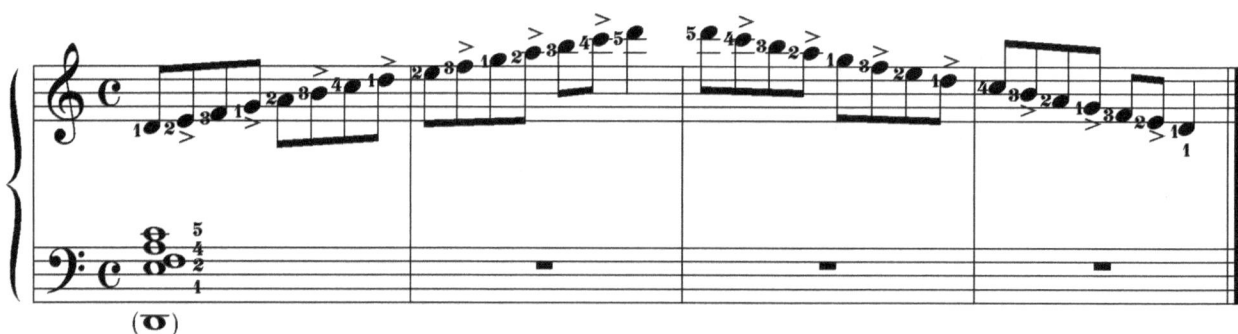

You can practice all of the scales and melodic ideas in this book using this technique of emphasizing the "upbeats". Remember, though, that this is just a practice technique. There is no one "rule" as to when to emphasize what notes. Your ability to feel weak beats as comfortably as strong ones is merely a prerequisite to eventually developing your own rhythmic style within a jazz context.

You may want to record yourself in order to better hear which of the above areas needs to be improved. Additionally, sound files containing each mode played as written below can be found on the Muse Eek website under this book's title. It is instructive to listen to the scales being played, and it can also be useful to play along, attempting to match the time feel and articulations as you do.

D Dorian Mode

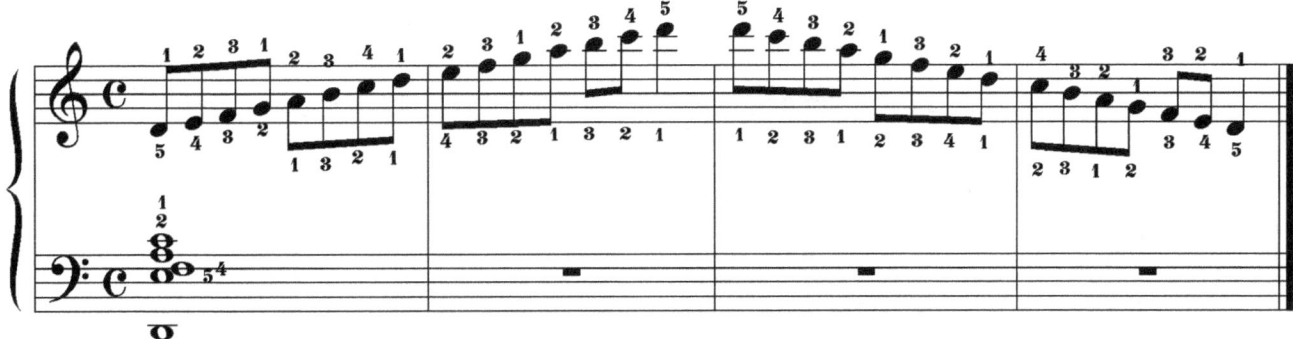

G Dorian Mode

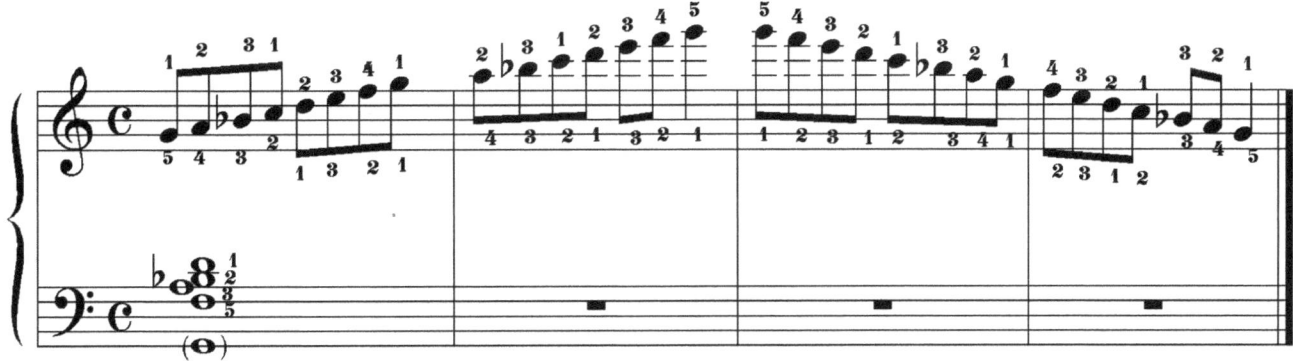

C Dorian Mode

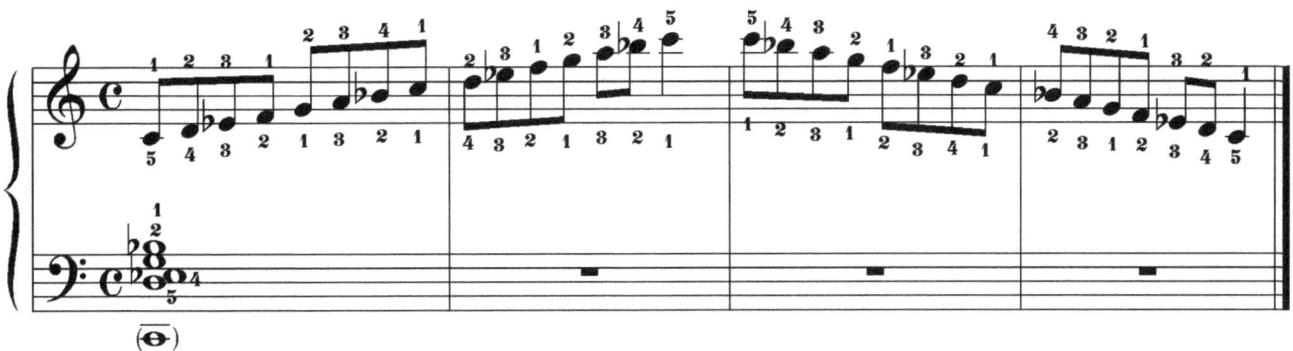

F Dorian Mode

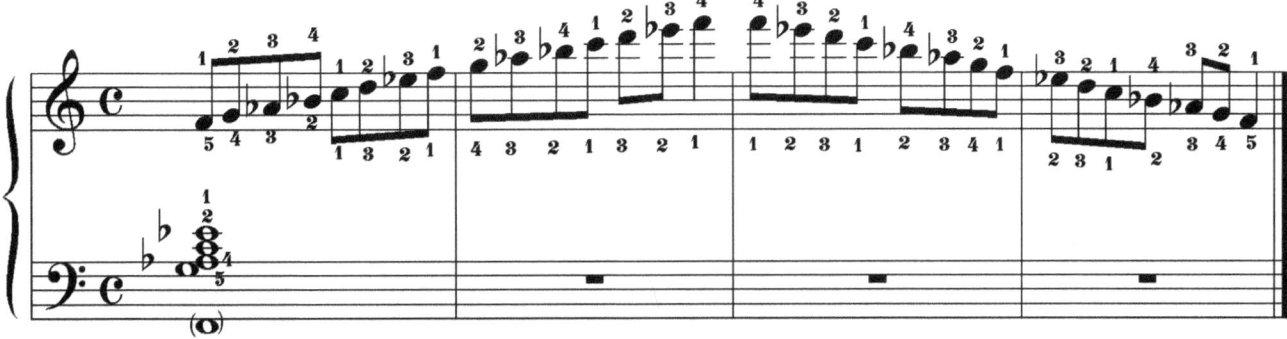

Bb Dorian Mode

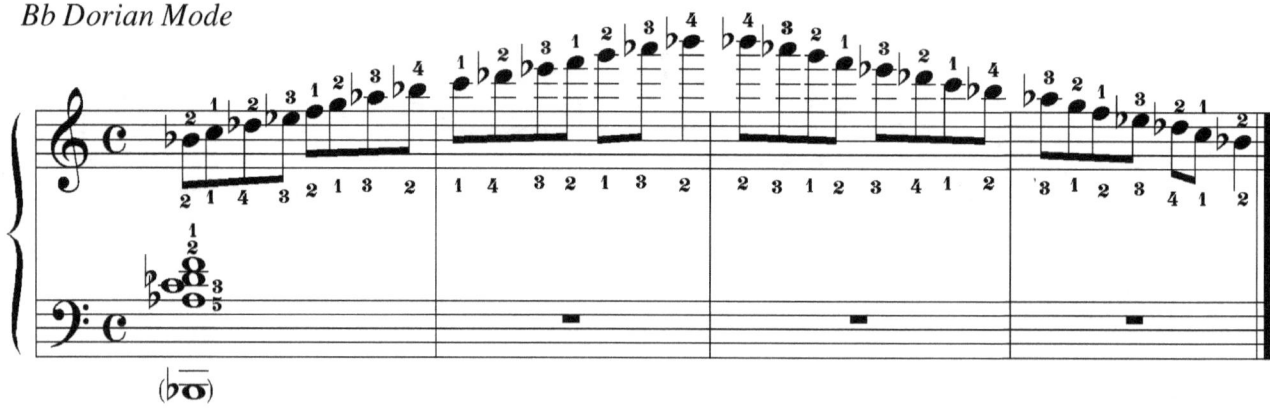

Eb Dorian Mode

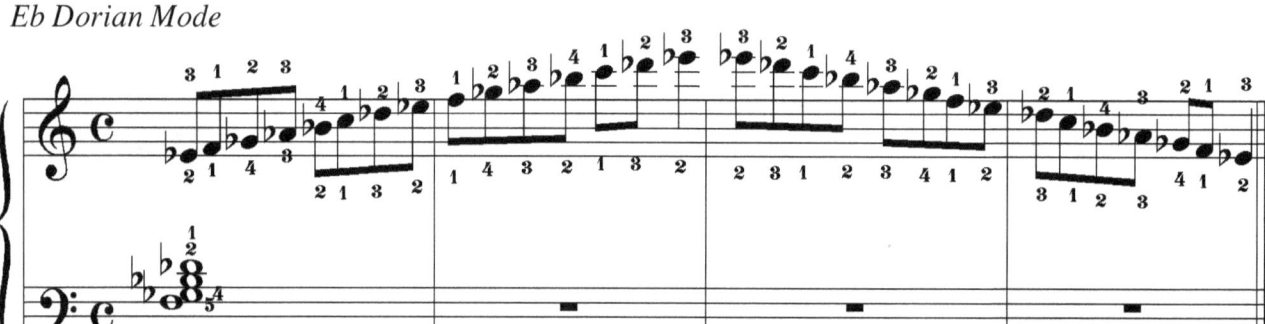

Ab Dorian Mode

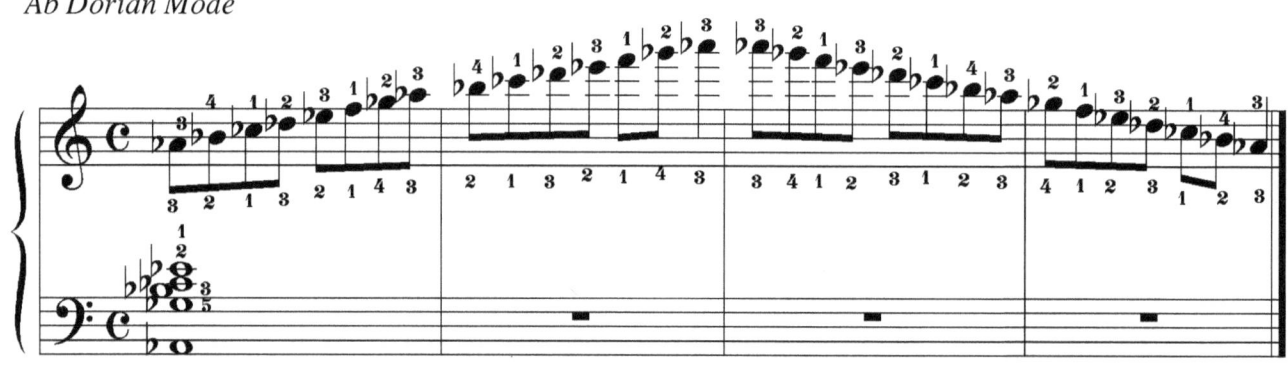

C# Dorian Mode

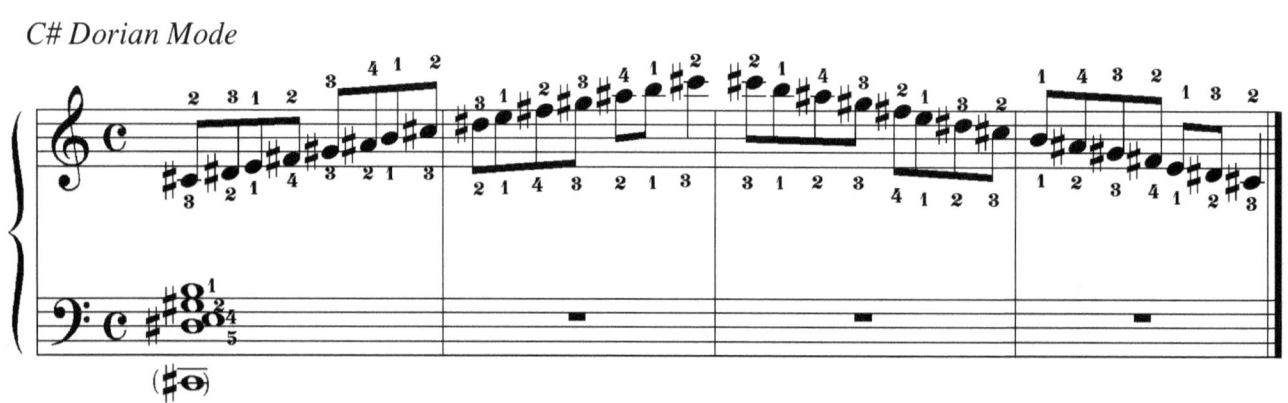

F# Dorian Mode

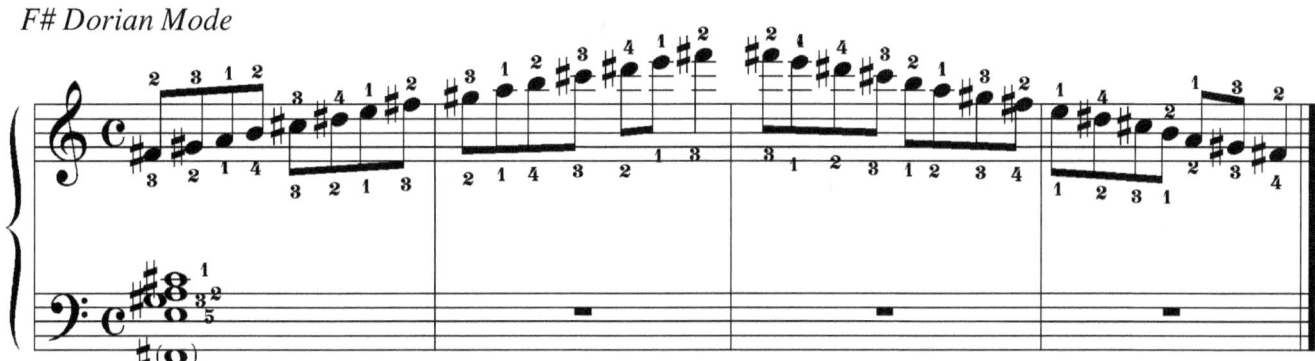

B Dorian Mode

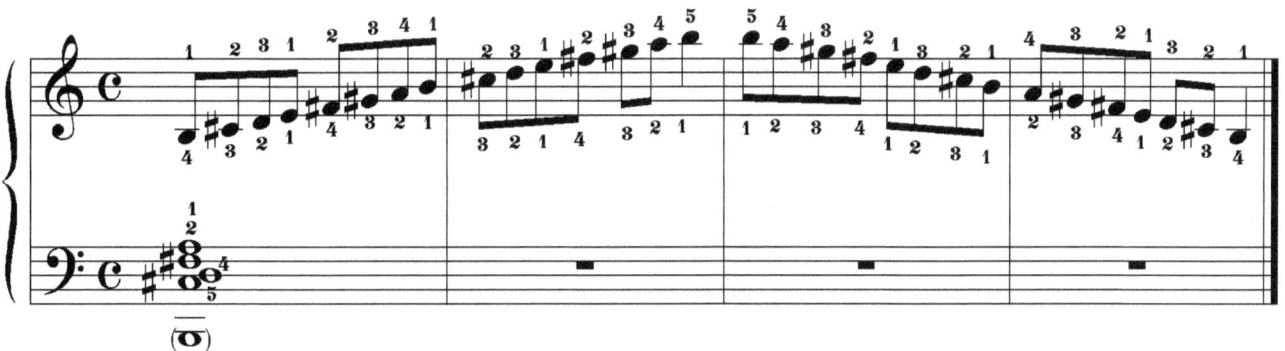

E Dorian Mode

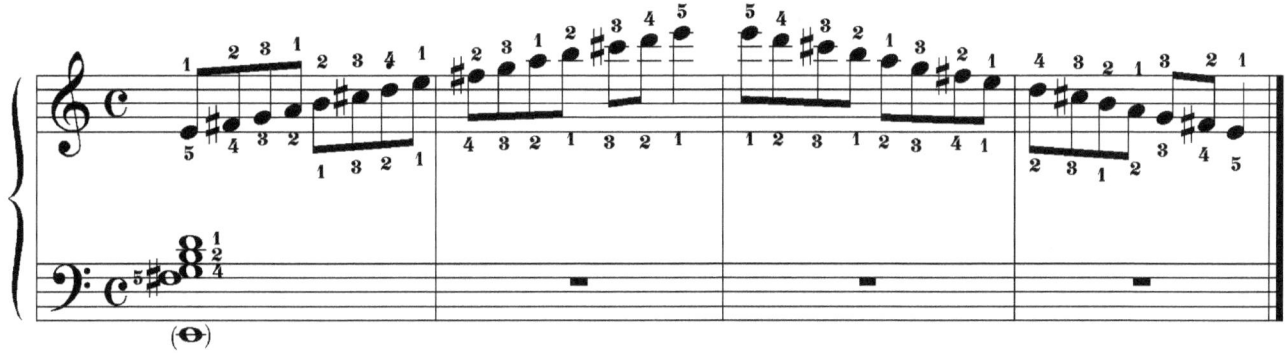

A Dorian Mode

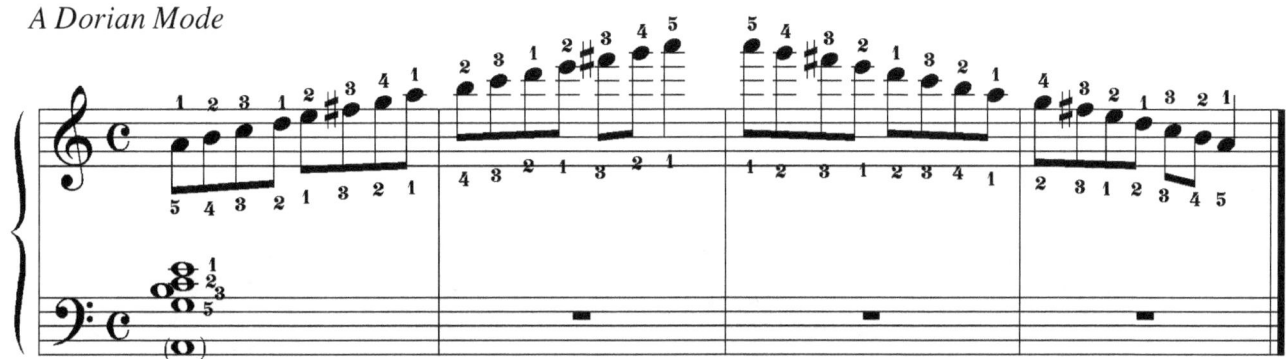

Other Ways To Practice The Dorian Mode

Exploring the same scales in different ways will help get the material into your ears and under your fingers. Towards that end, here are some suggestions for other ways to practice the Dorian modes. Audio files of all the examples in this section are available at the Muse Eek website under this book's title.

Modal Sequencing

Modal sequencing is defined as repeating the same melodic pattern as you ascend or descend a given scale. For example, a sequence using thirds over a D Dorian mode could consist of each note of the mode followed by the note that is a third above it:

Example 3

(Note that the fingering indicated for this particular example is only one of several options that will work well.)

Remember that whether to play a major third or a minor third is determined by which note is in the mode you are using. Thus, the same sequence of thirds played over an A Dorian mode would look like this:

Example 4

Suppose instead of a third we choose the interval of a fourth. Sequencing through an Eb Dorian Mode in fourths would look like this:

Example 5

Again, pay attention to the sharps or flats so that you are certain you are playing only the notes that are in the scale you are using.

Of course, we can use a pattern consisting of more than just two notes. Here we build on each note of C Dorian using two consecutive thirds to form a sequence of triads:

Example 6

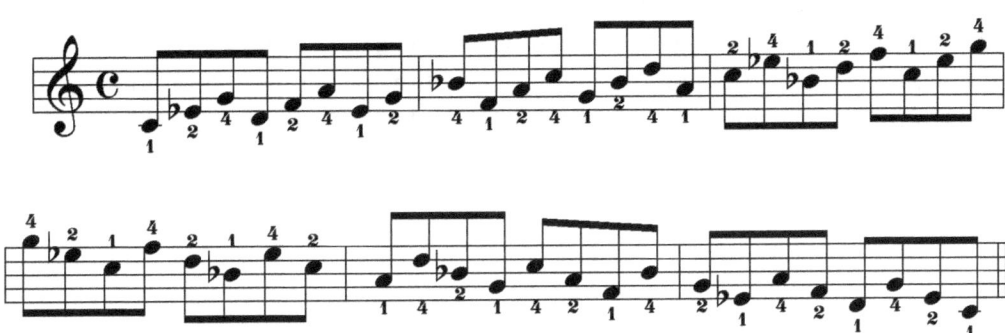

Below is an E Dorian modal sequence using a pattern consisting of a fourth followed by a third. This creates a sequence of arpeggiated (broken) triads in second inversion. (*Second inversion* means that the root of each triad is in the middle of the chord, not on the bottom):

Example 7

In the following sequence, the order of the second and third notes in the triads has been inverted:

Example 8

As you can see, the possibilities for creating interesting patterns are endless. Bear in mind that patterns are not a substitute for creating memorable melodic ideas. However, in addition to helping you learn scales and modes, patterns can help you learn to organize and achieve greater control over your melodic material, leading to greater clarity in your playing.

Intervallic scales

Another way to work on scales is to consider the possibility of the scale tones moving in intervals other than seconds. For example, instead of playing each mode stepwise, try playing the mode moving up in thirds. To begin, let's take a D Dorian mode. We start on D, but instead of going up the next step to E, we go up a *third* to F. From F, we go up a third to A. From A, we go up a third to C. We continue up in thirds until we arrive back at D, and then descend the same way, giving us:

Example 9

Let's look at this process using another mode, this time F Dorian, which has three flats (Bb, Eb and Ab). From F, we go up a third to Ab. From Ab, the next third would be C, followed by Eb, etc:

Example 10

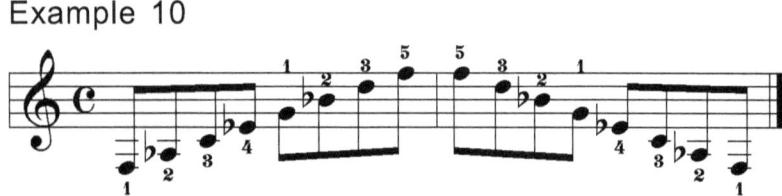

You can use this same intervallic concept to play a scale in fourths instead of seconds or thirds. Here is a D Dorian scale as it would be played in fourths. The fingering shown in these examples will work for all the Dorian modes when they are played using the same intervals.

Example 11

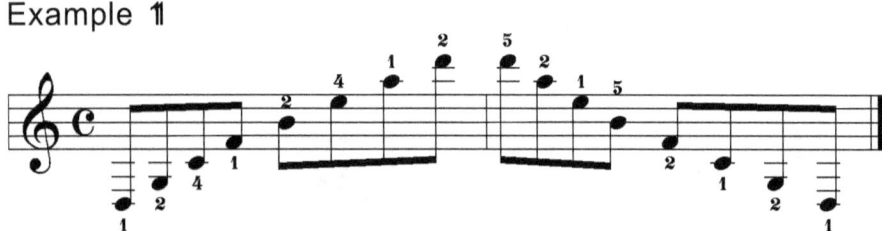

Here is an F Dorian mode played in fourths:

Example 12

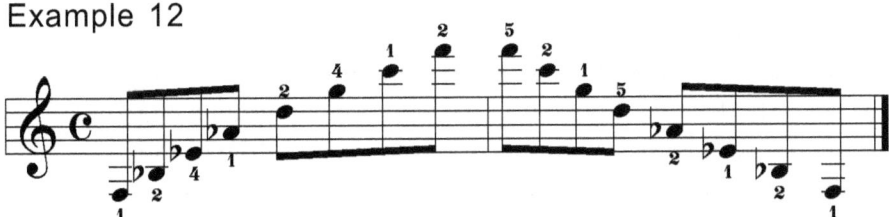

Try playing the modes, or any scale you happen to be working on, using these and other intervals (fifths, sixths or sevenths). As you apply this concept with wider intervals, it becomes more challenging. You will find that, in addition to enhancing your knowledge of the scale, it will greatly open up your ear to interesting melodic possibilities and will improve your ability to get around the keyboard as well.

Examples of Melodic Lines Using the Dorian Mode

After you have mastered the Dorian modes, you will want to try improvising using this new melodic vocabulary. A multitude of examples of melodic jazz lines derived from the Dorian mode have been provided to get you started thinking melodically. Even though a different melodic idea is given for each key, try to play each line in several different keys. This will help you better understand the relationship between the notes and the chord, which will improve your assimilation of the material. Transposing the lines yourself is always best, but if you have trouble with this the transpositions are provided on the Muse Eek website in the members area. Sound files of the examples below are also located on the Muse Eek website under this book's title.

Example 13

Example 14

Example 15

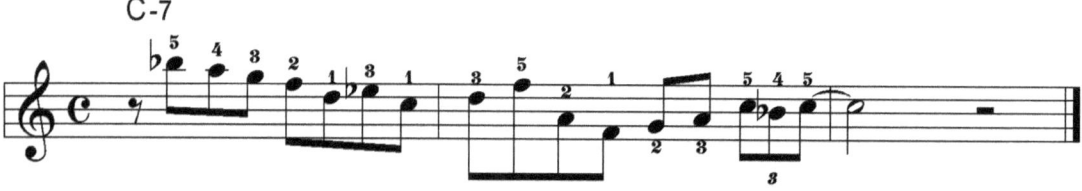

Example 16

Example 17

Example 18

Example 19

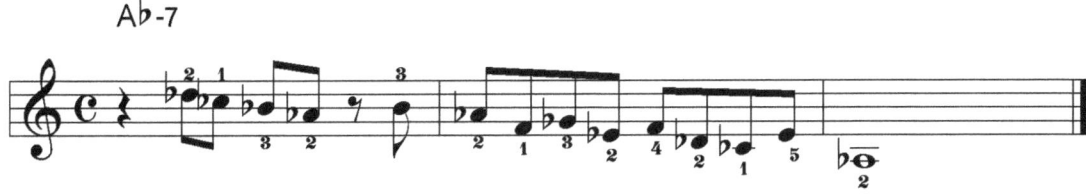

Example 20

Example 21

Example 22

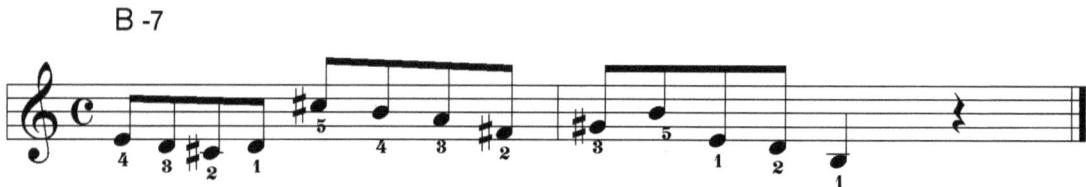

Example 23

Example 24

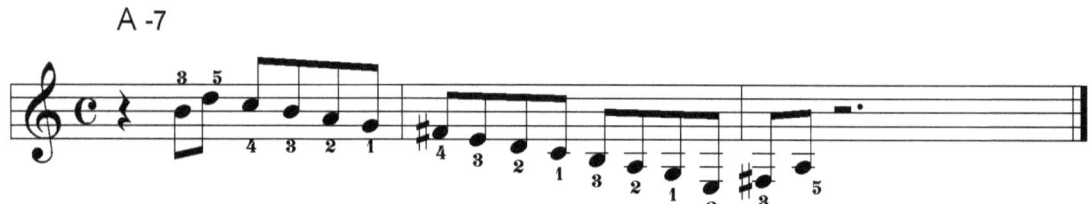

Your Ideas

On the following pages space is reserved for you to create your own melodic lines using the Dorian mode. Writing out your ideas slows down the process, allowing you time to better understand what you are doing. Another advantage of writing down your lines is that over time you will have a written record of your improved understanding of these concepts.

The goal of all this is, of course, to be able to improvise comfortably using this new vocabulary. Towards this end it is important to do *some* improvising every day. Even if you can only play a D Dorian scale to begin with, you should try improvising over it. At first it may not sound good to you, but that's what practice is for.

"Avoid" Notes

As you become a more fluent improvisor, you will become increasingly aware that in many scales there are certain notes which do not sound appropriate to the chord, particularly if you over-emphasize them. These notes are called the *avoid notes* of the scale. *Avoid notes* are defined as those non-chord tones which must resolve.

The Dorian mode contains no absolute *avoid notes*; however, if you play other styles of music besides jazz, you may wish to note that the sixth degree of the scale played against a minor seven chord has a "jazzy" sound that might not be appropriate in a non-jazz setting such as rock or pop music.

For example, in a D Dorian mode, the sixth degree is B:

If we emphasize the sixth degree, the minor seven chord starts to sound like a minor seven (thirteen) chord.

Example 25

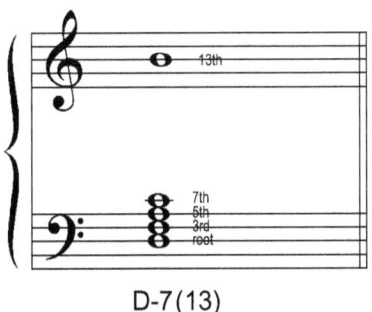

D-7(13)

Again, while this sound is fine or even desirable in a jazz context, the use of this chord in pop music would depend on how "jazzy" the music is intended to be.

When you write out and play your own practice lines on the blank staves below, try experimenting with emphasizing different notes in the scales in order to explore how the various color tones effect the mood and sound of the music. Which notes sound more "bluesy" to you? Which notes sound "brighter" or "darker"? There are no right or wrong answers to these questions. Your goal should be to develop and refine your ear and your personal taste.

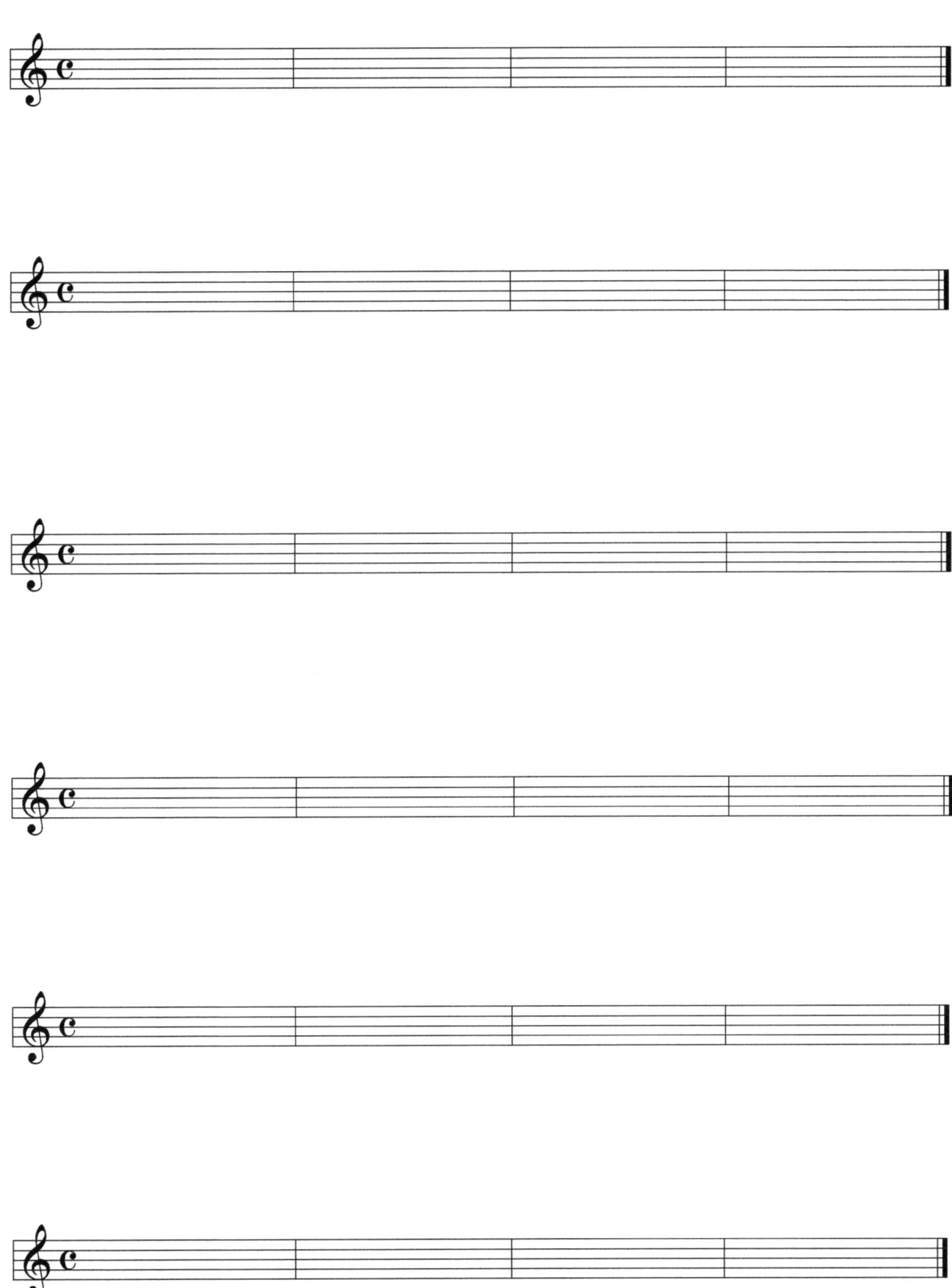

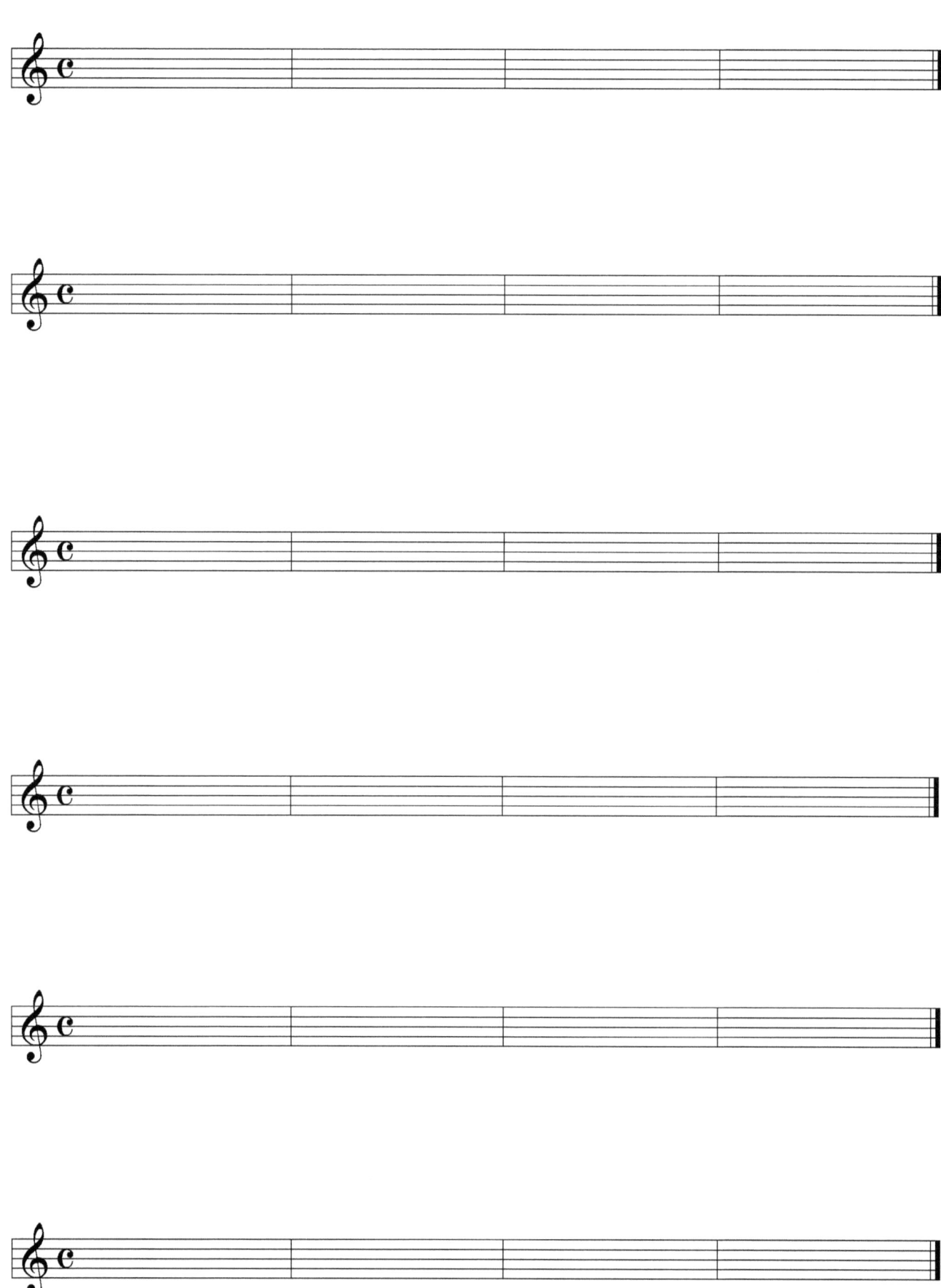

A Jazz Etude On *So What* Changes

The chord progression used in the following piece is often referred to as *"So What" changes* because these chord changes were used in Miles Davis' classic modal tune, "So What". (John Coltrane's composition, "Impressions", uses this very same chord progression.) This piece is an original etude which uses the D Dorian and Eb Dorian modes over D-7 and Eb-7, respectively.

After learning this piece, you can practice improvising over these chord changes; transpose the melody into other keys; write a piece of your own using Dorian modes...the practice possibilities are endless.

To hear the piece, download the audio file located on the Muse Eek website under this book's title. This piece is Example 26.

Example 26

What's That?
A Dorian Mode Etude

R. Piket

Further Exploration

Listening

I am always amazed when a student who wishes to learn to play jazz piano acknowledges that he or she rarely or never actually listens to jazz! Trying to play jazz without listening to the music is like trying to write a book without ever having read one. You must listen to the music you want to learn to play in order to understand what you are trying to accomplish. Eventually you will want to find your own style, but before you can do that, imitation and assimilation of the masters is critical.

Towards that end I have assembled a list containing some of the definitive jazz piano recordings of the past as well as some inspiring examples from the present. This list is not intended to be comprehensive, as that would require an entire book in itself. Rather, it is a cross-section of various styles from early jazz to contemporary jazz. It also reflects my own biases and preferences. If one of these pianists grabs your ear, then seek out other recordings by that pianist.

If you hear something you like, try to figure out what is being played and learn to play it. This will help you develop both your ears and your jazz vocabulary. There is no better way to learn than through primary source material. Listen to as much good jazz as possible.

Also keep in mind that much can be learned from listening to instrumentalists other than pianists. The CDs listed on the following pages are an excellent starting point because all of the musicians on those CDs, not just the pianists, represent some of the best on their respective instruments.

Cross Sectional Jazz Piano Discography

Early Jazz and Swing
Jelly Roll Morton: The Piano Rolls (Nonesuch)
Errol Garner: Concert by the Sea (Columbia)
Art Tatum: Solo Masterpieces (Volumes 1-7) (Pablo)
Mary Lou Williams: The Zodiac Suite (Smithsnian Folkways)

Big Band
Duke Ellington: The Feeling of Jazz (Black Lion)
Duke Ellington: And His Mother Called Him Bill (RCA/Bluebird)
Count Basie: Count Basie and His Orchestra (Circle)
Count Basie and Duke Ellington: First Time: The Count Meets the Duke(Columbia)

Be-bop
Thelonious Monk: Plays Duke Ellington (Original Jazz Classics)
Thelonious Monk: With John Coltrane (Original Jazz Classics)
Bud Powell: The Amazing Bud Powell (Volumes 1&2) (Blue Note)
The Quintet (with Bud Powell): Jazz at Massey Hall (Original Jazz Classics)
Bud Powell: Genius Of Bud Powell (Verve)

Post-Bop

Hard-Bop/Funky Jazz
Art Blakey and the Jazz Messengers (with Bobby Timmons): Moanin, (Blue Note)
Horace Silver: Cape Verdean Blues (Blue Note)

Modern Jazz
Red Garland: A Garland of Red (Original Jazz Classics)
Miles Davis (Red Garland): Milestones (Columbia)
Miles Davis (with Wynton Kelly): In Person - Friday and Saturday Nights at the Blackhawk
Miles Davis (with Bill Evans and Wynton Kelly): Kind of Blue (Columbia)
Bill Evans: Sunday at the Village Vanguard (Original Jazz Classics)
Bill Evans: You Must Believe In Spring (Warner Bros.)
John Coltrane (with McCoy Tyner): My Favorite Things (Atlantic)
John Coltrane (with McCoy Tyner): Giant Steps (Atlantic)
Ahmad Jamal: At the Pershing (MCA/Chess Jazz)
Phineas Newborn: A World of Piano! (Original Jazz Classics)
Lennie Tristano: Lennie Tristano/The New Tristano (Atlantic Jazz)

Post-Modern and Beyond
John Coltrane (with McCoy Tyner): A Love Supreme (Impulse)
Miles Davis (with Herbie Hancock): Nerfertiti (Columbia)
Miles Davis (with Herbie Hancock): Miles Smiles (Columbia
Herbie Hancock: Speak Like a Child (Blue Note)
Herbie Hancock: Maiden Voyage (Blue Note)
Herbie Hancock: Inventions And Dimensions (Blue Note)
Herbie Hancock: Headhunters (Columbia)
VSOP (with Herbie Hancock): The Quintet (Columbia)
Wayne Shorter (with Herbie Hancock): Speak No Evil (Blue Note)
Herbie Hancock and Wayne Shorter: 1 + 1 (Verve)
McCoy Tyner: The Real McCoy (Blue Note)
Chick Corea: Now He Sings, Now He Sobs (Blue Note)
Chick Corea & Return to Forever: Light as a Feather (Polygram)
Cecil Taylor: Unit Structures (Blue Note)
Keith Jarrett: The Koln Concert (ECM)
Charles Lloyd (with Keith Jarrett): Forest Flower (Rhino Records)
Marian McPartland: In My Life (Concord)
Marian McPartland: From This Moment On (Concord)
Fred Hersch: Heartsongs (Sunny Side)
Joanne Brackeen: Live At Maybeack Recital Hall (Concord)
Richie Beirach: Elegy for Bill Evans (Storyville)
Richie Beirach: Elm (ECM)
Richie Beirach and David Liebman: Chant (Creative Music)
Stanley Cowell: Live At Maybeack Recital Hall (Concord)
Jim McNeely: Group Therapy (Omnitone)
Renee Rosnes: Life On Earth (Blue Note)

By The Author
Roberta Piket & Alternating Current: I'm Back In Therapy And It's All Your Fault (Thirteenth Note)
Roberta Piket: September of Tears (Meldac)
Roberta Piket Trio: Midnight In Manhattan (Meldac)
Roberta Piket Trio: Speak, Memory (Fresh Sound/New Talent)
Roberta Piket: Live At The Blue Note (Half Note Records)
Roberta Piket: Unbroken Line (Criss Cross)

What Next?

If you have worked through this book you should be comfortable playing over minor seven chords using the Dorian mode. Of course, there is more to playing jazz than learning the "right notes". Your ears, your touch, your phrasing, and your sense of time (not to mention your heart and your head) are just a few of the areas that are important to you in becoming a good jazz player. You may wish to look at some of the online material in the members area of the Muse Eek website which includes some left hand comping rhythms, left hand fingerings for the Dorian modes, a brief treatise on hand position, and other helpful information.

This book is part of a series of books that focuses on learning and applying jazz scales in order to give you the vocabulary and confidence to become a fluid jazz improvisor. When you are ready, you may wish to build on the progress you've made by choosing another book in this series. Since dominant seventh chords are very prevalent in jazz and blues, you may wish to jump to Volume 5, *The Mixolydian Mode*. Or, if you prefer to go in order, you can proceed to Volume 3, *The Phrygian Mode*. Both of these books contain the applicable mode with fingerings in all twelve keys as well as melodic ideas, left hand chord voicings, and more.

Books Available From
Muse Eek Publishing Company

The Bruce Arnold series of instruction books for guitar are the result of 20 years of teaching. Mr. Arnold, who teaches at New York University and Princeton University has listened to the questions and problems of his students, and written forty books addressing the needs of the beginning to advanced student. Written in a direct, friendly and practical manner, each book is structured in such as way as to enable a student to understand, retain and apply musical information. In short, these books teach.

1st Steps for a Beginning Guitarist
Spiral Bound ISBN 1890944-90-4   Perfect Bound ISBN 1890944-93-9

"1st Steps for a Beginning Guitarist" is a comprehensive method for guitar students who have no prior musical training. Whether you are playing acoustic, electric or twelve-string guitar, this book will give you the information you need, and trouble shoot the various pitfalls that can hinder the self-taught musician. Includes pictures, videos and audio in the form of midifiles and mp3's.

Chord Workbook for Guitar Volume 1 (2nd edition)
Spiral Bound ISBN 0-9648632-1-9   Perfect Bound ISBN 1890944-50-5

A consistent seller, this book addresses the needs of the beginning through intermediate student. The beginning student will learn chords on the guitar, and a section is also included to help learn the basics of music theory. Progressions are provided to help the student apply these chords to common sequences. The more advanced student will find the reharmonization section to be an invaluable resource of harmonic choices. Information is given through musical notation as well as tablature.

Chord Workbook for Guitar Volume 2 (2nd edition)
Spiral Bound ISBN 0-9648632-3-5   Perfect Bound ISBN 1890944-51-3

This book is the Rosetta Stone of pop/jazz chords, and is geared to the intermediate to advanced student. These are the chords that any serious student bent on a musical career must know. Unlike other books which simply give examples of isolated chords, this unique book provides a comprehensive series of progressions and chord combinations which are immediately applicable to both composition and performance.

Music Theory Workbook for Guitar Series

The world's most popular instrument, the guitar, is not taught in our public schools. In addition, it is one of the hardest on which to learn the basics of music. As a result, it is frequently difficult for the serious guitarist to get a firm foundation in theory.

Theory Workbook for Guitar Volume 1
Spiral Bound ISBN 0-9648632-4-3   Perfect Bound ISBN 1890944-52-1

This book provides real hands-on application of intervals and chords. A theory section written in concise and easy to understand language prepares the student for all exercises. Worksheets are given that quiz a student about intervals and chord construction using staff notation and guitar tablature. Answers are supplied in the back of the book enabling a student to work without a teacher.

Theory Workbook for Guitar Volume 2
Spiral Bound ISBN 0-9648632-5-1   Perfect Bound ISBN 1890944-53-X

This book provides real hands-on application for 22 different scale types. A theory section written in concise and easy to understand language prepares the student for all exercises. Worksheets are given that quiz a student about scale construction using staff notation and guitar tablature. Answers are supplied in the back of the book enabling a student to work without a teacher. Audio files are also available on the muse-eek.com website to facilitate practice and improvisation with all the scales presented.

Rhythm Book Series

These books are a breakthrough in music instruction, using the internet as a teaching tool! Audio files of all the exercises are easily downloaded from the internet.

Rhythm Primer
Spiral Bound ISBN 0-890944-03-3   Perfect Bound ISBN 1890944-59-9

This 61 page book concentrates on all basic rhythms using four rhythmic levels. All examples use one pitch, allowing the student to focus completely on time and rhythm. All exercises can be downloaded from the internet to facilitate learning. See http://www.muse-eek.com for details

Rhythms Volume 1
Spiral Bound ISBN 0-9648632-7-8   Perfect Bound ISBN 1890944-55-6

This 120 page book concentrates on eighth note rhythms and is a thesaurus of rhythmic patterns. All examples use one pitch, allowing the student to focus completely on time and rhythm. All exercises can be downloaded from the internet to facilitate learning. See http://www.muse-eek.com for details.

Rhythms Volume 2
Spiral Bound ISBN 0-9648632-8-6   Perfect Bound ISBN 1890944-56-4

This volume concentrates on sixteenth note rhythms, and is a 108 page thesaurus of rhythmic patterns. All examples use one pitch, allowing the student to focus completely on time and rhythm. All exercises can be downloaded from the internet to facilitate learning. See http://www.muse-eek.com for details.

Rhythms Volume 3
Spiral Bound ISBN 0-890944-04-1   Perfect Bound ISBN 1890944-57-2

This volume concentrates on thirty second note rhythms, and is a 102 page thesaurus of rhythmic patterns. All examples use one pitch, allowing the student to focus completely on time and rhythm. All exercises can be downloaded from the internet to facilitate learning. See http://www.muse-eek.com for details.

Odd Meters Volume 1
Spiral Bound ISBN 0-9648632-9-4   Perfect Bound ISBN 1890944-58-0

This book applies both eighth and sixteenth note rhythms to odd meter combinations. All examples use one pitch, allowing the student to focus completely on time and rhythm. Exercises can be downloaded from the internet to facilitate learning. This 100 page book is an essential sight reading tool.
See http://www.muse-eek.com for details.

Contemporary Rhythms Volume 1
Spiral Bound ISBN 1-890944-27-0   Perfect Bound ISBN 1890944-84-X

This volume concentrates on eight note rhythms and is a thesaurus of rhythmic patterns. Each exercise uses one pitch which allows the student to focus completely on time and rhythm. Exercises use modern innovations common to twentieth century notation, thereby familiarizing the student with the most sophisticated systems likely to be encountered in the course of a musical career. All exercises can be downloaded from the internet to facilitate learning. See http://www.muse-eek.com for details.

Contemporary Rhythms Volume 2
Spiral Bound ISBN 1-890944-28-9   Perfect Bound ISBN 1890944-85-8

This volume concentrates on sixteenth note rhythms and is a thesaurus of rhythmic patterns. Each exercise uses one pitch which allows the student to focus completely on time and rhythm. Exercise use modern innovations common to twentieth century notation, thereby familiarizing the student with the most sophisticated systems likely to be encountered in the course of a musical career. All exercises can be downloaded from the internet to facilitate learning. See http://www.muse-eek.com for details.

Independence Volume 1
Spiral Bound ISBN 1-890944-00-9   Perfect Bound ISBN 1890944-83-1

This 51 page book is designed for pianists, stick and touchstyle guitarists, percussionists and anyone who wishes to develop the rhythmic independence of their hands. This volume concentrates on quarter, eighth and sixteenth note rhythms and is a thesaurus of rhythmic patterns. The exercises in this book gradually incorporate more and more complex rhythmic patterns making it an excellent tool for both the beginning and the advanced student.

Other Guitar Study Aids

Right Hand Technique for Guitar Volume 1
Spiral Bound ISBN 0-9648632-6-X   Perfect Bound ISBN 1890944-54-8

Here's a breakthrough in music instruction, using the internet as a teaching tool! This book gives a concise method for developing right hand technique on the guitar, one of the most overlooked and under-addressed aspects of learning the instrument. The simplest, most basic movements are used to build fatigue-free technique. Exercises can be downloaded from the internet to facilitate learning. See http://www.muse-eek.com for details.

Single String Studies Volume One
Spiral Bound ISBN 1-890944-01-7   Perfect Bound ISBN 1890944-62-9

This book is an excellent learning tool for both the beginner who has no experience reading music on the guitar, and the advanced student looking to improve their ledger line reading and general knowledge of each string of the guitar. Each exercise concentrates the students attention on one string at a time. This allows a familiarity to form between the written pitch and where it can be found on the guitar along with improving one's "feel" for jumping linearly across the fretboard. Exercises can be downloaded from the internet to facilitate learning. See http://www.muse-eek.com for details.

Single String Studies Volume Two
Spiral Bound ISBN 1-890944-05-X   Perfect Bound ISBN 1890944-64-5

This book is a continuation of Volume One, but using non-diatonic notes. Volume Two helps the intermediate and advanced student improve their ledger line reading and general knowledge of each string of the guitar. Each exercise concentrates the students attention on one string at a time. This allows a familiarity to form between the written pitch and where it can be found on the guitar along with improving one's "feel" for jumping linearly across the fretboard. Exercises can be downloaded from the internet to facilitate learning. See http://www.muse-eek.com for details.

Single String Studies Volume One (Bass Clef)
Spiral Bound ISBN 1-890944-02-5   Perfect Bound ISBN 1890944-63-7

This book is an excellent learning tool for both the beginner who has no experience reading music on the bass guitar, and the advanced student looking to improve their ledger line reading and general knowledge of each string of the bass. Each exercise concentrates a students attention of one string at a time. This allows a familiarity to form between the written pitch and where it can be found on the bass along with improving one's "feel" for jumping linearly across the fretboard. Exercises can be downloaded from the internet to facilitate learning. See http://www.muse-eek.com for details.

Single String Studies Volume Two (Bass Clef)
Spiral Bound ISBN 1-890944-06-8   Perfect Bound ISBN 1890944-65-3

This book is a continuation of Volume One, but using non-diatonic notes. Volume Two helps the intermediate and advanced student improve their ledger line reading and general knowledge of each string of the bass. Each exercise concentrates the students attention on one string at a time. This allows a familiarity to form between the written pitch and where it can be found on the bass along with improving one's "feel" for jumping linearly across the fretboard. Exercises can be downloaded from the internet to facilitate learning. See http://www.muse-eek.com for details.

Guitar Clinic
Spiral Bound ISBN 1-890944-45-9   Perfect Bound ISBN 1890944-86-6

Guitar Clinic" contains techniques and exercises Mr. Arnold uses in the clinics and workshops he teaches around the U.S.. Much of the material in this book is culled from Mr. Arnold's educational series, over thirty books in all. The student wishing to expand on his or her studies will find suggestions within the text as to which of Mr. Arnold's books will best serve their specific needs. Topics covered include: how to read music, sight reading, reading rhythms, music theory, chord and scale construction, modal sequencing, approach notes, reharmonization, bass and chord comping, and hexatonic scales.

The Essentials: Chord Charts, Scales, and Lead Patterns for the Guitar
Saddle Stitched (Stapled) ISBN 1-890944-94-7

This book is truly essential to the aspiring guitarist. It includes the most commonly played chords on the guitar in all keys, plus a bonus of the most commonly used scales and lead patterns. You can quickly learn all the chords, scales and lead patterns you need to know to play your favorite songs-and solo over them, too! "The Essentials" doesn't stop there, though. It also includes chord progressions to help you learn how to chord songs in folk, country, rock, blues and other popular styles. The books contain loads of easy to understand diagrams of chords, scales and lead patterns so you will be up and running in no time!

Sight Singing and Ear Training Series

The world is full of ear training and sight reading books, so why do we need more?
This sight singing and ear training series uses a different method of teaching relative pitch sight singing and ear training. The success of this method has been remarkable. Along with a new method of ear training these books also use CDs and the internet as a teaching tool! Audio files of all the exercises are easily downloaded from the internet at www.muse-eek.com By combining interactive audio files with a new approach to ear training a student's progress is limited only by their willingness to practice!

A Fanatic's Guide to Ear Training and Sight Singing
Spiral Bound ISBN 1-890944-19-X   Perfect Bound ISBN 1890944-75-0

This book and CD present a method for developing good pitch recognition through sight singing. This method differs from the myriad of other sight singing books in that it develops the ability to identify and name all twelve pitches within a key center. Through this method a student gains the ability to identify sound based on it's relationship to a key and not the relationship of one note to another (i.e. interval training as commonly taught in many texts). All note groupings from one to six notes are presented giving the student a thesaurus of basic note combinations which develops sight singing and note recognition to a level unattainable before this Guide's existence.

Key Note Recognition
Spiral Bound ISBN 1-890944-30-3   Perfect Bound ISBN 1890944-77-7

This book and CD present a method for developing the ability to recognize the function of any note against a key. This method is a must for anyone who wishes to sound one note on an instrument or voice and instantly know what key a song is in. Through this method a student gains the ability to identify a sound based on its relationship to a key and not the relationship of one note to another (i.e. interval training as commonly taught in many texts). Key Center Recognition is a definite requirement before proceeding to two note ear training.

LINES Volume One: Sight Reading and Sight Singing Exercises
Spiral Bound ISBN 1-890944-09-2   Perfect Bound ISBN 1890944-76-9

This book can be used for many applications. It is an excellent source for easy half note melodies that a beginner can use to learn how to read music or for sight singing slightly chromatic lines. An intermediate or advanced student will find exercises for multi-voice reading. These exercises can also be used for multi-voice ear training. The book has the added benefit in that all exercises can be heard by downloading the audio files for each example. See http://www.muse-eek.com for details.

Ear Training ONE NOTE: Beginning Level
Spiral Bound ISBN 1-890944-12-2   Perfect Bound ISBN 1890944-66-1

This Book and Audio CD presents a new and exciting method for developing relative pitch ear training. It has been used with great success and is now finally available on CD. There are three levels available depending on the student's ability. This beginning level is recommended for students who have little or no music training.

Ear Training ONE NOTE: Intermediate Level
Spiral Bound ISBN 1-890944-13-0   Perfect Bound ISBN 1890944-67-X

This Audio CD and booklet presents a new and exciting method of developing relative pitch ear training. It has been used with great success and is now finally available on CD. This intermediate level is recommended for students who have had some music training but still find their skills need more development.

Ear Training ONE NOTE: Advanced Level
Spiral Bound ISBN 1-890944-14-9   Perfect Bound ISBN 1890944-68-8

This Audio CD and booklet presents a new and exciting method of developing relative pitch ear training. It has been used with great success and is now finally available on CD. There are three levels available depending on the student's ability. This advanced level is recommended for students who have worked with the intermediate level and now wish to perfect their skills.

Ear Training TWO NOTE: Beginning Level Volume One
Spiral Bound ISBN 1-890944-31-9   Perfect Bound ISBN 1890944-69-6

This Book and Audio CD continues the method of developing relative pitch ear training as set forth in the "Ear Training, One Note" series. There are six volumes in the beginning level series. Through practice, the student eventually gains the ability to recognize the key and the names of any two notes played simultaneously. Volume One concentrates on 5ths. Prerequisite: a strong grasp of the One Note method.

Ear Training TWO NOTE: Beginning Level Volume Two
Spiral Bound ISBN 1-890944-32-7   Perfect Bound ISBN 1890944-70-X

This Book and Audio CD continues the method of developing relative pitch ear training as set forth in the "Ear Training, One Note" series. There are six volumes in the beginning level series. Through practice, the student eventually gains the ability to recognize the key and the names of any two notes played simultaneously. Volume Two concentrates on 3rds. Prerequisite: a strong grasp of the One Note method.

Ear Training TWO NOTE: Beginning Level Volume Three
Spiral Bound ISBN 1-890944-33-5   Perfect Bound ISBN 1890944-71-8

This Book and Audio CD continues the method of developing relative pitch ear training as set forth in the "Ear Training, One Note" series. There are six volumes in the beginning level series. Through practice, the student eventually gains the ability to recognize the key and the names of any two notes played simultaneously. Volume Three concentrates on 6ths. Prerequisite: a strong grasp of the One Note method.

Ear Training TWO NOTE: Beginning Level Volume Four
Spiral Bound ISBN 1-890944-34-3   Perfect Bound ISBN 1890944-72-6

This Book and Audio CD continues the method of developing relative pitch ear training as set forth in the "Ear Training, One Note" series. There are six volumes in the beginning level series. Through practice, the student eventually gains the ability to recognize the key and the names of any two notes played simultaneously. Volume Four concentrates on 4ths. Prerequisite: a strong grasp of the One Note method.

Ear Training TWO NOTE: Beginning Level Volume Five
Spiral Bound ISBN 1-890944-35-1   Perfect Bound ISBN 1890944-73-4

This Book and Audio CD continues the method of developing relative pitch ear training as set forth in the "Ear Training, One Note" series. There are six volumes in the beginning level series. Through practice, the student eventually gains the ability to recognize the key and the names of any two notes played simultaneously. Volume Five concentrates on 2nds. Prerequisite: a strong grasp of the One Note method.

Ear Training TWO NOTE: Beginning Level Volume Six
Spiral Bound ISBN 1-890944-36-X   Perfect Bound ISBN 1890944-74-2

This Book and Audio CD continues the method of developing relative pitch ear training as set forth in the "Ear Training, One Note" series. There are six volumes in the beginning level series. Through practice, the student eventually gains the ability to recognize the key and the names of any two notes played simultaneously. Volume Six concentrates on 7ths. Prerequisite: a strong grasp of the One Note method.

Comping Styles Series

This series is built on the progressions found in Chord Workbook Volume One. Each book covers a specific style of music and presents exercises to help a guitarist, bassist or drummer master that style. Audio CDs are also available so a student can play along with each example and really get "into the groove."

Comping Styles for the Guitar Volume Two FUNK
Spiral Bound ISBN 1-890944-07-6   Perfect Bound ISBN 1890944-60-2

This volume teaches a student how to play guitar or piano in a funk style. 36 Progressions are presented: 12 keys of a Major and Minor Blues plus 12 keys of Rhythm Changes A different groove is presented for each exercise giving the student a wide range of funk rhythms to master. An Audio CD is also included so a student can play along with each example and really get "into the groove." The audio CD contains "trio" versions of each exercise with Guitar, Bass and Drums.

Comping Styles for the Bass Volume Two FUNK
Spiral Bound ISBN 1-890944-08-4   Perfect Bound ISBN 1890944-61-0

This volume teaches a student how to play bass in a funk style. 36 Progressions are presented: 12 keys of a Major and Minor Blues plus 12 keys of Rhythm Changes A different groove is presented for each exercise giving the student a wide range of funk rhythms to master. An Audio CD is also included so a student can play along with each example and really get "into the groove." The audio CD contains "trio" versions of each exercise with Guitar, Bass and Drums.

Jazz and Blues Bass Line
Spiral Bound ISBN 1-890944-15-7   Perfect Bound ISBN 1890944-16-5

This book covers the basics of bass line construction. A theoretical guide to building bass lines is presented along with 36 chord progressions utilizing the twelve keys of a Major and Minor Blues, plus twelve keys of Rhythm Changes. A reharmonization section is also provided which demonstrates how to reharmonize a chord progression on the spot.

Time Series

The Doing Time series presents a method for contacting, developing and relying on your internal time sense: This series is an excellent source for any musician who is serious about developing strong internal sense of time. This is particularly useful in any kind of music where the rhythms and time signatures may be very complex or free, and there is no conductor.

THE BIG METRONOME
Spiral Bound ISBN 1-890944-37-8   Perfect Bound ISBN 1890944-82-3

The Big Metronome is designed to help you develop a better internal sense of time. This is accomplished by requiring you to "feel time" rather than having you rely on the steady click of a metronome. The idea is to slowly wean yourself away from an external device and rely on your internal/natural sense of time. The exercises presented work in conjunction with the three CDs that accompany this book. CD 1 presents the first 13 settings from a traditional metronome 40-66; the second CD contains metronome markings 69-116, and the third CD contains metronome markings 120-208. The first CD gives you a 2 bar count off and a click every measure, the second CD gives you a 2 bar count off and a click every 2 measures, the 3rd CD gives you a 2 bar count off and a click every 4 measures. By presenting all common metronome markings a student can use these 3 CDs as a replacement for a traditional metronome.

Doing Time with the Blues Volume One:
Spiral Bound ISBN 1-890944-17-3   Perfect Bound ISBN 1890944-78-5

The book and CD presents a method for gaining an internal sense of time thereby eliminating dependence on a metronome. The book presents the basic concept for developing good time and also includes exercises that can be practiced with the CD. The CD provides eight 8 minute tracks at different tempos in which the time is delineated every 2 bars, and with an extra hit every 12 bars to outline the blues form. The student may then use the exercises presented in the book to gain control of their execution or improvise to gain control of their ideas using this bare minimum of time delineation.

Doing Time with the Blues Volume Two:
Spiral Bound ISBN 1-890944-18-1   Perfect Bound ISBN 1890944-79-3

This is the 2nd volume of a four volume series which presents a method for developing a musician's internal sense of time, thereby eliminating dependence on a metronome. This 2nd volume presents different exercises which further the development of this time sense. This 2nd volume begins to test even a professional level player's ability. The CD provides eight 8 minute tracks at different tempos in which the time is delineated every 4 bars with an extra hit every 12 bars to outline the blues form. New exercises are also included that can be practiced with the CD. This series is an excellent source for any musician who is serious about developing an internal sense of time.

Doing Time with 32 bars Volume One:
Spiral Bound ISBN 1-890944-22-X   Perfect Bound ISBN Spiral Bound ISBN 1890944-80-7

The book and CD presents a method for gaining an internal sense of time thereby eliminating dependence on a metronome. The book presents the basic concept for developing good time and also includes exercises that can be practiced with the CD. The CD provides eight 8 minute tracks at different tempos in which the time is delineated every 2 bars, with an extra hit every 32 to outline the 32 bar form. The student may then use the exercises presented in the book to gain control of their execution or improvise to gain control of their ideas using this bare minimum of time delineation.

Doing Time with 32 bars Volume Two:
Spiral Bound ISBN 1-890944-23-8   Perfect Bound ISBN Spiral Bound ISBN 1890944-81-5

This is the 2nd volume of a four volume series which presents a method for developing a musician's internal sense of time, thereby eliminating dependence on a metronome.. This 2nd volume presents different exercises which further the development of this time sense. This 2nd volume begins to test even a professional level player's ability. The CD provides eight 8 minute tracks at different tempos in which the time is delineated every 4 bars with an extra hit every 32 bars to outline the 32 bar form. New exercises are also included that can be practiced with the CD. This series is an excellent source for any musician who is serious about developing an internal sense of time.

Other Workbooks

Music Theory Workbook for All Instruments, Volume 1: Interval and Chord Construction
Spiral Bound ISBN 1890944-92-0   Perfect Bound ISBN 1890944-46-7

This book provides real hands-on application of intervals and chords. A theory section written in concise and easy to understand language prepares the student for all exercises. Worksheets are given that quiz a student about intervals and chord construction using staff notation. Answers are supplied in the back of the book enabling a student to work without a teacher.

Jazz Piano Vocabulary by Roberta Piket, Volume 2: The Dorian Mode
Spiral Bound ISBN 1890944-96-3   Perfect Bound ISBN 1890944-98-X

This book is the 2nd volume in a series designed to help the student of jazz piano learn and apply jazz scales by mastering each scale and its uses in improvisation. Each book focuses on a different scale, illustrating the scale in all twelve keys with complete fingerings. Also provided are chords and left hand voicings to match, exercises and etudes to help apply the material to improvising, ideas for further study and listening, and detailed instructions and suggestions on how to practice the material.

E-Books

The Bruce Arnold series of instructional E-books is for the student who wishes to target specific areas of study that are of particular interest. Many of these books are excerpted from other larger texts. The excerpted source is listed for each book. These books are available on-line at www.muse-eek.com as well as at many e-tailers throughout the internet. These books can also be purchased in the traditional book binding format. (See the ISBN number for proper format)

Chord Velocity: Volume One, Learning to switch between chords quickly
E-book ISBN 1-890944-88-2

The first hurdle a beginning guitarist encounters is difficulty in switching between chords quickly enough to make a chord progression sound like music. This book provides exercises that help a student gradually increase the speed with which they change chords. Special free audio files are also available on the muse-eek.com website to make practice more productive and fun. With a few weeks, remarkable improvement by can be achieved using this method. This book is excerpted from "1st Steps for a Beginning Guitarist Volume One."

Guitar Technique: Volume One, Learning the basics to fast, clean, accurate and fluid performance skills.
E-book ISBN 1-890944-91-2

This book is for both the beginning guitarist or the more experienced guitarist who wishes to improve their technique. All aspects of the physical act of playing the guitar are covered, from how to hold a guitar to the specific way each hand is involved in the playing process. Pictures and videos are provided to help clarify each technique. These pictures and videos are either contained in the book or can be downloaded at www.muse-eek.com This book is excerpted from "1st Steps for a Beginning Guitarist Volume One."

Accompaniment: Volume One, Learning to Play Bass and Chords Simultaneously
E-book ISBN 1-890944-87-4

The techniques found within this book are an excellent resource for creating and understanding how to play bass and chords simultaneously in a jazz or blues style. Special attention is paid to understanding how this technique is created, thereby enabling the student to recreate this style with other pieces of music. This book is excerpted from the book "Guitar Clinic."

Beginning Rhythm Studies: Volume One, Learning the basics of reading rhythm and playing in time.
E-book ISBN 1-890944-89-0

This book covers the basics for anyone wishing to understand or improve their rhythmic abilities. Simple language is used to show the student how to read and play rhythm. Exercises are presented which can accelerate the learning process. Audio examples in the form of midifiles are available on the muse-eek.com website to facilitate learning the correct rhythm in time. This book is excerpted from the book "Rhythm Primer."

www.ingramcontent.com/pod-product-compliance
Lightning Source LLC
LaVergne TN
LVHW061319060426
835507LV00019B/2222